HUSTLENOMICS

    It's a hustle inside of you that, you may have not discovered yet, the hustle to achieve more than you ever imagined possible. I know you may be thinking, that you need no other hustles, because the one you have, has been working fine. But why spread yourself, so thin. In this game there is a "101" hustle's, why limit yourself to just one.

The go getters guide, can help you get versatile, and a lot of goals accomplished. It'll help you gain more respect, more money, more power and recognition. In this world wide hustle we are living in, only the person who isn't hustling, is only the person who isn't living. At some point, almost everybody hustles, different names, but all of it is the same. There is No Standing Still in the game. You must have a go getter's mentality, and if you don't, don't panic. Just apply this go getter advice to your hustle, and I promise, when the world seems to be collapsing around you, you and your hustle will remain solid as a "Rock", able to take on whatever the game throws your way.

The first concern for all people is "survival". In our society, we use money to meet our needs, and most people get these needs met by hustles. You earn money threw hustling. Freedom is money, nothing can replace freedom: being able to make decisions, shot call, control the destiny of your life, and to be free we must hustle. This means more than just selling dope, you can't be a hustler, and have a one tracked mind or you'll always find yourself in a position as a slave in the streets, always depending on someone else. When you have a variety of hustles, you always can depend on one; if by choice the other one goes bad. Hustling for a living is a normal part of life and will bring satisfaction. First we have to have a deep desire to hustle hard, its determination that makes a bonafide hustler. We have to constantly remind ourselves, that our short time in this world, we have the choice to be a "go-getter" or a "no getter". The choice to be the one that "make things happen" or the one that "watch things happen". I ain't sure about you, but I don't want to be the one living off frozen dinners. I want to be the one living off being an "winner". You know what I'm talking about. Most people choose to lose. Its as if they scared of money: which could be the case. Scared of all the responsibilities, having money brings. They're scared of the problems that comes along with having money. A lot of people fear, being the target. Not everyone loves the attention money brings, and when I say money, I don't mean chump change, I mean the type of money you can't hide. Everybody knows you have it. Everybody wants money. Its not a person on God's green Earth that can tell me they don't want money. They might not want the drama that surrounds the relationship with money, so they choose to mismanage money, carelessly spend it, give it away. Then once broke complain about not having any money. When this world calls upon them to get money and save it, what do they do? You guessed it, they trick it off on some bullshit, never crossing their mind to invest it into a project for a profit. I never really understood the average dope boy, they would cash out close to 20 thousand for a whip (car) with rims, music etc., but they are still living at home with mom. You don't buy a whip before you buy a house. That's an example of mismanagement of money, careless spending, unless a guy hook up a car for a certain amount of money and then sells it for a certain amount of money to make a profit. These guys don't do that. They ride the whip til the wheels fall off, until they're high off pills, drugs, or drunk and end up having an accident. They don't have insurance so that 15 to 20 thousand gone down the drain that he has to charge to the game. However its no big deal to a go-getter, we learn from our mistakes. We control the hustle, the hustle don't control us. We design our hustle, so that it's rewarding for our future. So stack that money high as you can, and remember the hustles out there can sometimes mean getting our hands dirty, even if it's a legitimate one. At one point or another, you will have to take some fucked up risks some risks that some aren't ready to take, but if a person doesn't have what he or she likes they must like what they have. We get out of our hustles what we put in our hustles. We shouldn't expect a damn thing, if we haven't made any sacrifices, so in other words hustling isn't all peaches and cream. It can get real deep. The morals and principles that you have in life will have to be set to the side, if you are a person that couldn't picture yourself lying, stealing, cheating then you can't picture yourself as a millionaire. You will have to sacrifice your good hearted nature to avoid becoming a victim in this race to the top. Best believe that they have plenty of people that will stomp on your fingers and kick you down the ladder of success. You will have to be just as cutthroat as they are. However, a lot of things in life is always easier said than done. One thing is for sure, you get ahead or fall behind according to how much knowledge, you have about the game of life. This book is overflowing with knowledge, so suck it up.

If you made it this far, I must say we have a lot in common, a blood hound thirst for the money. Hustle bones in the body, a strong will to make something out of nothing. The game is good to us that have it. I notice that if you take care of your hustle, your hustle will take care of you. If your stuck in the dope game don't be a stranger to change. If your stuck with a minimum wage don't settle for less, open new horizons to the American Dream. When you do what you have always done, you will get what you always gotten. Having a strong hustle isn't impossible if you want it, and if you got it already keep it. Deep thinking, hustlers with a serious minded approach will make something happen. It's something you will have to understand, even if you're a good hustler, you will never be a perfect one

HUSTLERS MOTIVATION

I think its hustle, or be hustled in this world. The game is full of people that would love to take you for everything you got. Every minute a hustler is born right along with a sucker, so it's just about the same amount of hustlers as there is suckers. Sometimes suckers can rub off on you. You can be a bonafide hustler but if you hang around suckers, you'll end up as one. I've seen plenty of go-getters lose their Mojo, from association with non hustlers. I'm a firm believer that you have to be SOLO at most hustles. You are never truly free to call yourself a bonafide hustler until you're able to come up by yourself. The strongest person in the world is the one who stands alone. Withdraw yourself from a crowd of hustlers, hustle by yourself it's not a coincidence that most self made millionaires are also loners. This is when you see that game from a bonafide hustler's perception.

However real hustlers are born with a built in radar that makes them no stranger to the expression of loyalty and commitment to the hustle. In this world wide hustle, we as go-getters, systematically have to develop a strategy, one by one, until we conquer the game. First we got to have an understanding about money and how it can come between the best of relationships, mother and son, wife and husband, and best of friends. How far will you allow money to control your life? Where do you draw the line to your hustle? Do you know the difference between money and true wealth? Money can be taken from you at anytime, but wealth is yours forever, wealth is your hustle. Nobody can rob you of experience and skills. We confuse having the best with being the best, no go getters usually measure themselves, by comparing their life to the saying "grass is always greener on the other side." This is a major distraction. You have to be content with your hustle. There will always be someone who seems richer, and more successful. What it comes down to is being able to develop our internal wealth, it's the safe that can't be cracked. I came to realize that money is not more important than a person. At the same time put yourself first, because no one will keep your own interests and goals firmly in mind and hustle hard to achieve them for you. Before we slide off to this next chapter, you must know in life most people become masters at dreaming about getting money, but in reality they choke when the opportunity presents itself. They become lost for words so in my next chapter of gift of gab I'll be breaking down some useful jewels for verbal and non-verbal communication is concerned. So follow me into the next chapter to get a hustlers eye view of the character it takes to have the gift of gab

GIFT OF GABB. SWAGG

In this chapter we are going to get in more detail about the Art of Hustling. To persuade another person to give you their valuable time, you need to offer something of value in return. First and foremost, that something will have to be your conversation. As in any part of life, in the world of hustling, you have to have strong command of words, and the skill of stroking egos. People are ego hungry and as long as you satisfy that hunger: you will have an open door to sell whatever to that person. People are more agreeable more understanding, and more cooperative if you feed his or her ego. Give that person a genuine compliment, or hell some insecure flattery, anything to make the sale. Try looking for little things you can compliment them about. Compliments open the minds of people who would otherwise tell you to go to hell. Not having conversation will be a serious handicap in this game. If you can't express yourself without hesitating about the right words to choose you are disqualified to sell anything to anybody. The most important key is the 5 "P"s, which is proper preparation prevents poor performance, and get knowledge about what you plan on selling ahead of time. You can be your own worst enemy. You can also talk your way in and or out of a sale. It can be a time where your talking good and you have got the prospect sold, but you continue to talk because you are feeling the gift of gab, the all of a sudden the prospect changes his or her mind, so you will have to know your own strength. The most successful hustlers are the ones that have a way with people. People are the key to our hustles. It's most that we learn how to master the knack of dealing with people, and part of this is having the skill of stroking egos. People are ego hungry and as long as you satisfy that hunger you will have an open door to sell whatever to that person. People are more agreeable, more understanding, and more cooperative if you feed his or her ego. You know give that person a genuine compliment, or hell some insecurity, flattery, anything to make the sell. But try looking for little things you can make a compliment about. Compliments open the minds of people who would otherwise tell you to go to hell if you approach them with something to sell. People are more interested in themselves than in anything else in the world and every person you meets want to feel important, so you take advantage of this and make them feel important. It takes nothing from you by doing so it's all game. Start addressing people by names such as: Chief, Boss, Big Guy, Captain, and you'll see the results in these labels. Your hustle will be smoother. The way we approach people in general is important, if you look at somebody before you approach them and decide that, that certain person is likely to be difficult to deal with, chance are they will. Trust your hunches; don't confuse your hunches with wishful thinking. However, you will have to approach this person in a manner which he will accept you can never sell anything to anybody until you sell yourself first. The person is almost forced into buying what you are selling. Confidence is the key at accomplishing this goal. You can make others have confidence in you and your proposition, by acting confident. All the greatest hustlers know how important confidence is. The art of acting as if it was impossible to fail to make a sale. A confident manner in a go-getter is like having money in the bank. Let people know that you expect to win. Hold up your head, look the person in the eyes, walk as if you had a million dollars in your pockets. If you believe in yourself and act as if you believe in yourself, others will have no choice but to believe in you, even if all of what you say is not sure.

On the flip side of things being able to recognize a customer's confidence can be a valuable asset. The customer with an air of confidence might not be an easy sell, but I can almost guarantee you that the customer without confidence in themselves will be an easy target. Its little things that give customers away, lack of confidence has a way of showing itself in clearer ways. Their acceptance will appear on their face, common sign are in the way they walk, they might walk with their head down, eyes to the ground and steps hesitant as if he or she were scared to let go, and step out. It's important to recognize these traits in order to know what kind of prospect you are dealing with. Another clue is the way a prospect you are dealing with shakes hands with you. The way is he or she shakes hand tells you far more than what you expect. These clues are not anything I have made up, its psychology, the laws of nature. The limp, type of handshakes, displays lack of confidence in what you plan to sell them. A firm shake is what you are looking for. It basically says, I'm alive, I've got a firm grasp of things and I like your proposal. This can also be a way to tell if a person is agreeable with your first impression. Shake a prospect hand upon meeting him or her and see what kind of response you get. This leads me to first impressions:

First Impression

In order to have a gift of gab work for you, you have to have a gift of appearance. The way we dress plays a major role in our hustle, it affects your sales. The power of first impression is making it your best impression because you never get a second chance to make a first impression. The way you dress, the way you walk, the way you smile is the important factor in the game. Look as if you were successful and you'll get treated as if you were successful even if in fact you are not. Look as if you are the shit and you'll get treated as if you are shit.

The very first words out your mouth are important. If you begin by clowning around with a person it is hard to convince that person later on down the line to take you serious. If you want a person to take you serious sound serious in your very first words. If you want it to be business like, start off in a business like tone. Automatically a person would rise to the occasion he or she will act the role that you set out. People tend to accept you at your own evaluation, if you act like a king, you will be treated like a king. Act like a nobody, you'll get treated like a nobody, in this hustle to the top nobody is handed down the game on a platinum platter. This book is the closest you can get to getting a hand out, but you have to make the hustle your hustle. If someone hands it to you for free I wouldn't take it, because the person that handed it down to you, will ask of a price of you in return. Nothing for free in this world and everybody's looking for something, so it's always a hustle to be made. Having a strong hustle is holding your own, anything less is form of slavery. Develop that gift of gab, make that first good impression. Enter the room of social interaction, with your eyes wide open, your game face on, ready to sell water to a well, and ice in hell. Hustling means to be alert, on top of the game. It means recognizing the needs of the people with whom you will be dealing with to be a go getter you must size up life situations and stay persistence in your hustle, speaking of persistence in your hustle, speaking of persistence let get a little deeper into what it takes.

Persistence

    The gift of gab goes right along with being persistent. Persistence is real important in your hustle, because a lot of people tend to give up on their gift of gab, after being rejected by a prospect. You have to remember you could never please every person; at least 40% of the people you come in contact with will disagree with you. The positive thing is you will always have a 60% chance, at getting someone to buy whatever idea you plan to sell. Don't ever get discouraged by a customer or person you're trying to sell an idea too, if they don't buy what you're talking about just look at it as his or her loss. Let it be known that you can never escape this fact no matter how good you think your gift of gab is, you can fool some of the people some of the time, but not all of people, all of the time. I got that quote from the president. I forgot which one. However much you attempt to sell always remember not to invest your own self worth in its success or failure. So if somebody doesn't buy what you are selling don't get emotionally tied to what you plan to sell. It's all business nothing personal. With this in mind it will help you to stay persistent, and it help your conversation, when a prospect says no, it doesn't mean take no as a answer. It just means that you have to present your proposition in a different choice of words and fashion. Make promises, make guarantees, and use any tactic besides giving up. Appeal to the prospects greed. Using greed to your advantage is the most important tool. Greed makes anything easier to believe. A con artist uses this tactic the most and is very successful at it, because he knows that people are always greedy for gain. Greed is people's down fall. People are infatuated with a creative hustler, so be creative with your approach, don't come with the same lines, be unique. For example; let's say you are a door to door sales person. A female answers the door, you say "I hate to bother you ma'am" or "I won't take up much of your time." These lines are tired, and without your knowledge to it you are giving her a role to act out in from you setting the stage, where she only acts as a person who is being bothered and whose time is being taken up. A go-getter will be unique in his approach. It's what makes the gift of gab the gift of gab. Before you try to sell anything you have to ask yourself the question what do I really want? How do I want this to go? What mood do I want to display, this all plays a major role in hustling, in this world the conversation runs the nation before I close this chapter I'm going to encourage you to increase your vocabulary, your word play to be able to paint a picture with words inside a prospects head that he or she can visualize and accept the true gift of gab.

Chapter #:
Dope Boy Magic

When I say hustler, the first thing pops into your mind is a dope boy. From a lot of people point of view, the dope game looks like one big party. If I was to ask you what does a dope boy do?, you'd probably tell me that he drives a cool whip, parties, make a lot of easy money, and has all the women and do whatever he can possibly ask for. He's boss! A go-getter and your somewhat right. What about the rest of it? The part you don't see, that happens behind the scenes. The shady characters that's waiting for the perfect time to rob him and the blow his brains out, or the feds that are waiting for perfect time to snatch him off the streets for a decade or more. People that don't understand the dope game call it easy money. Just because it looks easy from the outside looking in, but once you see from a street perspective you find out that it isn't easy at all. That's what I'm going to do, let you see the game from the street's perspective. A street hustler never really amounts out to much, because they choose to sell themselves short. A lot of them possess the skills, that it takes to be a millionaire but they choose to waste this talent on street dreams and every time you look around they are back and forth from the joint (prison) for petty dope cases. This is what you call hustling backwards. I myself played the dope game for awhile, so I can't really knock the hustle. Guys out there don't think ahead of time. They don't care to find out, why they are hustling dope. What am I hustling for? How long will I stay hustling? How much money is enough? Should I put some money away in case I get jammed? These are the questions you have to ask yourself in the dope game. Whether you're flipping sacks or maintaining a legitimate business. You will need money for two things a good lawyer, and the best deals or products. It's a golden rule. That if you save your cash, your cash will save you. It doesn't matter what kind of hustle you choose, either legal or illegal the more money you have the more money you'll have the ability to make. Money makes money. Most guys out there in the dope game always fail to save their money. It goes to gambling, clubs, partying, making it rain, playing the big shot on the block, buying cars and tricking off with women. Until every dime has been spent on bullshit. This is not the example of a real hustler, a real hustler would think futuristically, real-estate would be on his or her mind. Buying a business to wash the money would definitely be one of his or her main priorities. Every successful hustler we have ever met had a vision inside them, deep down they believe that they can do anything, be the best and lead the way. They can see a three million dollar dynasty. They light up when they talk about money. You must know how to take a risk. Successful hustlers take risks, but they usually take measured risks. A odds of the worst case scenario has been examined and bound to be acceptable. You can't accept getting your head blown off over some chunky with substance nor could you accept being in the fed joints for ten or more years. I'm going to tell you know you mess around and be forgotten in that place. The dope game is deep and while I'm on the subject of it being deep I want to break down the snitching aspect of it all.

SNITCHES

Now a days snitching has become a fad. It seems like it's the thing to do. Why do ten when you can give it to a friend. From hood to hood guys are snitching on each other. It's impossible to protect yourself from a snitch. You can say, I'll just serve only the people that I know, but the people you know is the ones doing the shipment is to be distributed in a chain of command, first to the CIA and then to the FBI to guys in the good that work for the FBI which we call snitches or just plain employees of the FED jail. The bottom rank is the ones they recruit by black mail. I won't give you that much time, if you take down so and so "but although it's a dirty game so call it fair that we are subject to entrapment, and in the face of every warning, and every prison term we still choose to contribute to their plan to destroy our race. We need to use our resources more wisely. I know most of us don't plan on hustling this way for the rest of our life. I know most of the dope games as a stepping stone to establishing some kind of legitimate business. Too feel like a productive member of society, so it's not that we sell dope to cause intentional harm to anybody, but they hand out prison time like we do. A lot of times our backs are against the wall. Very few jobs that would be considerate enough to hire a felon in spite of his skills to do the job. It's like they can't look past the past, and give the opportunity to work, to create a positive attitude in our life. And the average guy on the streets, know that if you don't work you don't eat. That alone leaves a guy with little if any choice and end up taking the risk of going to prison. It's either that or starves on the streets. Which will you choose? I know you probably thinking that that's what family support is for, but in the hood family support is at all time low. More than likely they're situation isn't in any better shape than he has or she has. Then guys are faced with their kid's mother down their back, demanding financial assistance for the kids. When she knows damn well he don't have a job, and he's barely providing for himself. So she adds to the stress and so you feel less than a man not being able to look out for you and yours. So to rebuild your self worth you consider doing the most convenient thing for you to accumulate instant money. The thing we know best is selling dope seem like a necessity to survive. We neglect the knowledge of the consequence for getting caught. Knowing that these people will try to throw the book at us. It wasn't until I was up and age, that it crossed my mind that I was fed up with selling dope in doing time. Hopefully I can save you some time, so it wont take you that many years to understand, that you can make some real cash without working a square job, without having a college degree, without having to go to the joint and without risking your life for them crumbs in the streets. I just want you to know that you can create a legitimate hustle set your own hours and be your own boss. This mean if you're willing to hustle hard, put in the time, get the knowledge you need out this book, and hustle as hard for yourself as you did on the street, you can write your meal ticket, without the bullshit. If you want to live long and prosperous in this game of life, you have to do more than sell dope or whatever street level hustle you are doing, its got to stop. It's not the prime example of a go-getter. A go getter is willing to try shit that hasn't been done before. If you're on the street hustling, you are hustling backwards, this mean you put your money, your freedom, and life on the line. This is what the average guy does in this game. To be a go getter, you have to think outside the box, hustle above the circumstances of the moment. A go getter would never limit his or her game. This means you cannot be afraid to learn their language in dress their style, in just play the game. You have to be able to adapt, and learn how to communicate in all types of situations with all types of people this is what you call an all around hustler. The ability to customize your hustle is important. If you sell dope more than likely you are a good talker, quick decision maker, a born leader, and a boss. The person that makes things happens. So make things happen. The game is constantly saying to you, either plan to get it right or plan to fail. You better believe they got a plan for us, within the legal system they pass laws everyday that we are not aware of until it's too late. We are living in modern day slavery. Unlike in the past, it was done by physical force, they want us to believe that the American dream is within selling dope. America was never meant to be a luxury for us they promised a new way of life: each individual a free man, each having the right to seek his or her own happiness. It was all a dream. If we continued to chase these street dreams we are going to fall into their trap. To alter our existence as hustlers, like Jeezy said "You can play the game it's ok to floss, but its only one rule playa don't get caught"!

HOW TO SURVIVE WITHOUT THE DOPE GAME

Our generation is fascinated with the dope game it's the life! Niggas get a rush from making that money. But the feds get a rush from making that indicting us. This shit I'm about to kick will teach you how to break the cycle and invest that dope money into the corporate world. It's time to stop playing games you see these white folks aren't playing with us, it's time to wise up and get legit.

We got to understand that we got more to lose than to gain in the dope game. If you think about it the average nigga gets a three year run before he gets popped off and end up doing 6 years in the joint for three years worth of shine. If that. Ask niggas that was having millions from the game, but now in the feds if they could do it all again. They tell you they would of wash them hands and invested that money in a legitimate establishment. Some might tell you they they wish they never sold a crumb. It's not that the dope game isn't good to niggas, all the money, cars, clothes, and hoes is intoxicating and addictive. You got to know when to stop. After getting money with that, in fact that would be smart if you learn how to chase this corporate money with the same drive you have for the dope game. See the game serves one purpose and that to get ahead start in life, not to wait around for the inditement list.

Unfortunately niggas do just that, my goal is to help you cheat the dope game and beat the feds. Although some niggas play it smart by going legit, but most fall victim to the trap. That's why you got to realize enough is enough. It's hard to be satisfied with money, because you gone always want more. Just as fast as your money grows your needs grow and that's where niggas fuck up at the mix needs up with wants. Basically, what comes down to is being able to establish a limit. When you get enough for the a crib and a business sit your ass down and live off of that, or live in the joint around a gang of niggas for the next five to ten or more this the shit niggas got to think about. The game is a trap design by the government they milking niggas for they youth. They know it, your bitch know it, and you might as well know it. The game is in bad shape, niggas snitching including the plug. Its popular now to rat on your nigga to avoid the bid. It's considered being slick and smart, we all know its risky business and the dope game is like a gamble, just like a gamble you're bound to crap out in lose without a doubt.

The dope game is the big inside joke: the only people who find it fascinating is the on whom didn't get a change to experience it firsthand. The better approach is to put niggas up on game. Teach them some business skills like self presentation, leadership, money management, computer conscious, savy real-estate invesments, stocks, bonds, and shit like that the shit we gone be focusing on in this book. I'll be breaking this shit down in the easy way possible, so you can understand the many ways of getting money legit. It's so much money to be made, that you'll be mad at yourself for not being hip earlier in the game. I mean free money, other people's money how the fuck can you go wrong if you use these tools I'm about to bless you with.

You got to see this shit happening for you got to visualize the outcome you want you got to start with a plan and set priorities. You gota ask yourself do I need it or do I want it? In the dope game we say "we need" shit that we actually don't "need"."Need" is shit we got to survive on. "Want" is shit that make life interesting and fun like the 28" rims, you need a place to stay, but you want a candy colored whip. This takes back to priorities everybody has wants, but we need to put needs come first. You need to own your crib before you cash out on a whip with rims. When it comes to money you have to respect it. You don't go around making it rain for no bitch, you risking your life for that cash don't be foolish, stack your shit. Take a break from buying fits every day, popping pills and drinking Remy and Patron. Stop buying shit that depreciates with time. Stack that money stop playing these big shot games, and get real. Invest in you bills to build your credit. Get your credit score together, so when you go hall to the bank they can trust you with 50 stacks knowing you can pay it back because you keep up with your bills. Make that money you work for you don't blow that shit back into the streets. The dope game just a mean of ends. Not the end itself. Don't roam the game aimlessly, make a plan you'll know where you want to go. You'll have a better chance of getting there stacking, which is the most important thing you can do to reach that plan. Put that money away and you'll be thankful that you did.

Banging and Booming

In this chapter I'll be breaking down the game in a step by step fashion. It covers all the aspects of getting your business banging and booming. Everything is a presented from licensing, to book keeping to marketing to setting up shop. Top notch advice from a boss hustler.

The chapter is for you if you're through with the dope game, or if you're just looking for some game. To start your own business and want to get things done the way they are supposed to be done. You've had the dream of owning your own hustle for a while now but you didn't have the blue print now you do. Starting a business can seem overwhelming without a blue print; it's so much to do, so much to figure out. Like how to set prices? What licenses you need? How do you choose a location? Where do you find customers? Where do you get the money? All this can make you say the hell with owning a business, but that won't be the case, because I will be breaking the game down to you in a simple to do fashion. Certified hustlers describe themselves as visionaries because they can see into the future of that grand hustle they have put down. They in vision their business banging and booming. The Benz, Jaguars, condos, and mansions. A hustler wants to leave their mark, they are not just striving to make a living but to leave a legacy.

Bossing up

If you're serious about being a Boss Hustler, chances are you've the type of person who like make things happens. You have a lot of energy, and I take it you have places to go, people to see, and things to do, which means you put your hustle muscle into whatever you plan to achieve.

When you're going into business for yourself you need to become an expert at lot of things in a very short time. That's alright who could you possibly trust do the job more than yourself. When you're not working, you're not making money. The only person that controls your work flow is you. When you work for yourself the line between work and life can be thin. At first you might feel good about hustling hard, all day, all night; on the weekends but it to will be a time where you ask yourself where my life is. Thats the price you have to pay for being the boss. A good boss is able to set goals for his workers make decisions and explain the purpose of the plan clearly. You must act as a coach and keep your emotions in check. Most of all you must be a creative hustler. Boss hustlers also know that people can only reach their potential when they are motivated to do so.

Once you declare yourself as a boss. Your body language, dress, and speech must become more upscale. This can be a problem if you are use to thugging with the white tees, Nike Air Max, and a due rag. I know if you switch your style up you'll get a lot of criticism from the guys. Some of it can be hard to take considering that your pride yourself as being still a street nigga. Here is the things you will have a corporate hustle going for yourself, which forces you to speak the English language correctly, being hoes can be tricky, don't hire friend or relatives, there is no way you can deal with them on a professional level when they make mistakes on purpose, like not showing up for work or coming late ect. Here's a motto to follow. Never mix family and friend, remember, your workers can make you or break you. If you cannot motivate your workers to produce good work you will be behind in your hustle, you are only going to get as much as you give. Don't expect giving this out, you being a boss you should never lie to your workers. Don't make promises you can't keep. Don't be scared to admit when you're wrong. Don't criticize your workers in front of anyone. People do much better work when they know what is expected of them. Make sure your orders are clear. Things do go wrong and your workers are only human so they will make mistakes when call some in your office to talk about how they have messed up keep your emotions in check. You can make it to the top of the corporate America hustle. Not a problem, but don't forget that there are thousands of guys in the hood still trying to make it. Remember where you came from. You can be your greatest friend or your biggest enemy. While most people let the games control them. Your mission is to take control of the game. You're either in control or out of control. In this game whatever can go wrong will go wrong at the worst possible time. You become truly on top of your game when you learn how to be yourself on top or bottom. Experience is the best teacher, so get out there and experience the game. To be a boss you have to have a mindset that allows you to be a leader .

www.ingramcontent.com/pod-product-compliance
Lightning Source LLC
Chambersburg PA
CBHW051826170526
45167CB00005B/2175